MW00964711

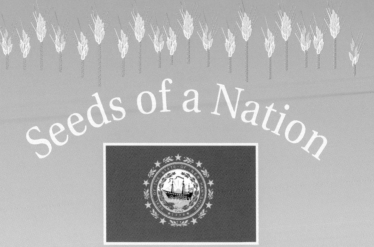

Seeds of a Nation

New Hampshire

Sheila Wyborny

KIDHAVEN PRESS™

THOMSON
——— ✦ ———™
GALE

San Diego • Detroit • New York • San Francisco • Cleveland
New Haven, Conn. • Waterville, Maine • London • Munich

THOMSON

GALE

On cover: Colonists sort their belongings at Odiorne's Point—New Hampshire's first settlement.

© 2003 by KidHaven Press. KidHaven Press is an imprint of The Gale Group, Inc., a division of Thomson Learning, Inc.

KidHaven™ and Thomson Learning™ are trademarks used herein under license.

For more information, contact
KidHaven Press
27500 Drake Rd.
Farmington Hills, MI 48331-3535
Or you can visit our Internet site at http://www.gale.com

LIBRARY OF CONGRESS CATALOGING-IN-PUBLICATION DATA

Wyborny, Sheila, 1950–
    New Hampshire / by Sheila Wyborny.
    v. cm. — (Seeds of a nation)
    Includes bibliographical references and index.
    Contents: The land and its earliest people—The arrival of the Europeans—Decades of conflict—Revolution and statehood.
    ISBN 0-7377-1448-4 (alk. paper)
    1. New Hampshire—History—Colonial period, ca. 1600–1775—Juvenile literature. 2. New Hampshire—History—1775–1865—Juvenile literature. [1. New Hampshire—History—Colonial period, ca. 1600–1775. 2. New Hampshire—History—1775–1865.] I. Title. II. Series.
    F37 .W94 2003
    974.2'02—dc21   2002013946

Printed in China

Contents

Chapter One

The Land and Its Earliest People

New Hampshire is in the northeastern United States. It is bordered on the east by Maine and Vermont to the west. Massachusetts is New Hampshire's southern neighbor, and it shares its northern border with the Canadian province of Quebec.

New Hampshire has three geographic regions. The coastal lowlands, located in the southeastern corner of the state, are made of sand beaches, salt marshes, and meadowlands. The eastern New England upland is a large area that covers more than half the state. It has lakes, hills, and river valleys with rich soil for farming. It also has granite, gravel, and mica quarries. The White Mountains cover the northern third of the state. This area includes the Presidential range and the Franconia range. Mount Washington, in the Presidential range, has set records for the highest recorded winds in the United States on its highest peak of 6,288 feet.

This land was shaped about fourteen thousand years ago as glaciers (huge masses of ice) retreated northward. Slowly, as the climate warmed, the rivers, lakes, and woodlands developed.

The First People

The earliest people of this land, called Paleo-Indians, appeared about nine thousand years ago. They had followed mastodons and wooly mammoths into this region. After about seven thousand years, with the gradual

Mastadons lived thousands of years ago in the state now known as New Hampshire.

warming of the climate, these large animals from a colder climate became extinct. As the larger game disappeared, the Paleo-Indians began hunting smaller animals, such as deer and elk. The people continued to move about the region, hunting and gathering.

A later group, known to have lived in this region around 2000 B.C., became known as the Red Paint People. They were given this name many years later by scientists because of their custom of lining burial pits with a mineral called red hematite. Archaeologists believe that red, like the color of blood, was a sacred color to these people.

The next period of the early people of North America began about 1000 B.C. and lasted into the time that Europeans discovered North America.

People of the Dawnland

During that time, one of the main Native American groups living in the area now known as New Hampshire was called the Western Abenaki. Abenaki means "people of the dawnland." The Abenaki were a part of a larger group, the Algonquian, which inhabited the area we know today as New England.

The dense woods and plentiful fish and game provided food, clothing, and shelter for these people of the woodlands. The Abenaki gathered apples, wild strawberries, roots, mushrooms, and nuts. Trees provided shelter, canoes, storage, and musical instruments. Waterways yielded an abundant supply of fish, and the dense woods provided game.

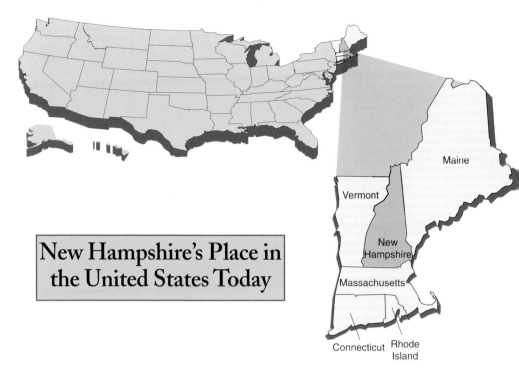

New Hampshire's Place in the United States Today

Maine

Vermont

New Hampshire

Massachusetts

Connecticut Rhode Island

Although their environment provided for their needs, working for food, shelter, and safety kept the Abenaki people quite busy.

Men's and Women's Roles in the Community

Abenaki women were busy from morning until night. They planted and harvested crops. The crops included corn, squash, and pumpkins. Another crop they planted was tobacco, which was used for special ceremonies and as a pain killer. The women also prepared the food, took care of the children, tended the fires, and tanned animal hides. If the village needed to be moved, the women packed all the belongings and did much of the carrying to the site of the new village. The villagers moved to follow herds and other available food sources.

A Native American man builds a canoe out of tree bark.

The men cleared the land at the new village site, built the homes, carved the canoes, built the animal traps, hunted for food, and protected the village from enemies.

Even the members of the community who were too old to tend crops or hunt helped out. They carved tools, sewed nets for fishing, and made the clay pots for storing food and hauling water.

People on the Move

Although the Abenaki raised crops for food, they also depended on game and fish for part of their diet. If game and fish in an area became scarce, the village packed and moved.

The need to be able to follow game meant that their homes could not be permanent structures. They had to be easily taken apart, carried, and reassembled on the new village site. Because of this, they built wigwams, round one-room shelters made of wood frames and covered by animal skins or tree bark. Skins sheltered the

Abenaki build wigwam shelters using wood frames and animal skins.

wigwams from harsh winter winds. Each wigwam had a smoke hole in the center of its ceiling to vent the smoke from the fire in the center of the room. Wigwams had raised platforms around the interior walls. These platforms kept families off the cold ground in the winter.

Because the Abenaki were used to moving when an area no longer had game and fish, they believed that people did not actually own the land. Rather, people used it until it was time to move on. This belief later led to serious problems, and finally wars, with people who arrived on the shores from distant lands.

Chapter Two

The Arrival of the Europeans

The area now known as New Hampshire, as well as the rest of New England, provided an abundance of natural resources for the Indians. When European explorers arrived along the upper Atlantic coastline and journeyed inland, they were amazed by this plentiful supply of natural resources. The explorers saw this new land as a potential source of wealth that could be exploited for their home countries. They returned home with stories of dense forests, fish, and game.

Explorers from England

The first man to sail the coast of New Hampshire was Martin Pring, an English sea captain. Pring sailed the northeast coast from what is now Maine to Massachusetts. Along the way, he sailed inland up the mouth of the Piscataqua River. He also discovered the Isles of Shoals, nine islands located six miles off the coastlines of Maine

and New Hampshire. Over time, these islands received colorful names: Star, Duck Island, Cedar, Appledore, Malaga, Lunging, White, Seaveys Island, and Smutty-nose. These islands became part of New Hampshire.

Pring was followed in 1614 by Captain John Smith. Following Smith's exploration of the area, he wrote a book titled *A Description of New England*. Upon reading Smith's account, King James I of England was so impressed that he granted a charter to the Council of New England, a group of noblemen in England who set up and governed the colonies in New England. By the authority of the charter, the council financed the founding of the colonies in New England. It planned transportation and supplies for future colonists, and it planned for surveying and assignment of parcels of land to the colonists.

In 1632 three other Englishmen, Captain Walter Neale, Darby Field, and Henry Jocelyn explored the inland area of New Hampshire. Their goals were to find gold and precious stones and to establish fur trade with the Indians. They reached the mountain range now known as the White Mountains before running dangerously low on supplies and having to turn back. All they found for their hardships were some worthless crystals, tales of a huge three-hundred-mile mountain range, and a forbidding land of dark forests beyond it.

And during this time explorers from other European countries traveled the shoreline of this corner of North America. Some of these explorers claimed many of the same discoveries as the Englishmen.

Italy

Giovanni Verrazano was an Italian navigator and explorer. Backed by King Francis I of France and Italian bankers and merchants, Verrazano sailed east in 1524 on his ship, *Dauphine*, with his fifty-man crew and his brother, Girolamo, a mapmaker, hoping to discover a route to the Pacific Ocean. What they found instead was an uneven coastline and red-skinned, powerfully built people, dressed in grasses and animal skins. Although Giovanni Verrazano was the first to see New York Harbor and Narragansett Bay, he did little actual exploring of the inland region. When Verrazano did look closer at an area that interested him, he would anchor his ship offshore and send a party onshore in a small boat. He did not want to risk the safety of the ship and the entire crew in an unknown area. Although the ship was safer offshore,

Italian explorer Giovanni Verrazano and his party land in New England's Newport Harbor.

the trip onshore could be dangerous. The shore party never knew what they might encounter on land. But Verrazano's caution did not save him.

On an expedition across the Atlantic Ocean in 1528, Verrazano went ashore with a landing party on an island near Florida. The group was attacked and killed by natives. The natives were cannibals, or people who eat human flesh. Only Verrazano's brother, who had remained on the ship, survived.

But despite danger and hardship, explorers from other countries also set their sights on the New World.

France

French explorer Samuel de Champlain accompanied several expeditions to the northeastern coast of North America beginning in 1603. Champlain made his first journey to the New World as an observer under Captain Francois Grave du Pont. Champlain wrote his book, *The Savages,* based on his observations of the wild new land.

From 1604 to 1607 Champlain made other voyages to the New World. During these expeditions, Champlain made maps of the New England coast from the Saint Croix River in the north to Cape Cod in the south. His maps included the Isles of Shoals, for which his expedition also claimed discovery.

In 1608 Champlain led an expedition to the New World, bringing French settlers with the intention of starting a colony. Champlain and his settlers called their settlement Quebec. They sailed down the Saint Lawrence River and all the way to the Great Lakes, establishing a

Rafts travel the rapids of the Saint Lawrence River. French explorer Samuel de Champlain sailed down the river and established trade with the Indians.

trade network with the Indians. Champlain's twenty-five-year leadership secured the control of the Saint Lawrence River and established a strong bond between the French and the Indians of North America. This relationship later involved the Indians in a bloody war between the French and the English in New England.

John Mason's Land Grant: New Hampshire

One of the parcels of land granted by King James I went to English merchant John Mason. Mason and his associate, Sir Ferdinando Gorges, received an unclearly defined, poorly described parcel that became

King James I of England (pictured) granted the present-day state of New Hampshire to merchant John Mason.

the present-day states of Maine and New Hampshire. Mason named his portion, the land between the Merrimack and Piscataqua Rivers, New Hampshire after his home county in England. Mason wanted to establish New Hampshire settlements that were fur trading posts and fishing villages. In fact, he invested a large sum of his own money in clearing land, building homes, and providing for New Hampshire's defense.

Mason made many plans for his parcel of land, but he did not see those plans carried out. Although Mason intended to sail to New Hampshire and was, in fact, making preparations for his trip in 1635, he died without ever setting foot on American soil. Although Mason never saw the land he named, many colonists braved the difficult journey to settle there.

A Settler's Life

Settlers came to New Hampshire for a variety of reasons. Some came seeking a place they could freely practice their religious beliefs.

One such group was led by Reverend John Wheelwright, a Puritan minister. He was branded a heretic, someone whose beliefs differed from the fundamentals of the church. Because of his beliefs, Wheelwright was banished from Massachusetts Colony and he and his followers founded Exeter, New Hampshire.

New Hampshire had four coastal communities by 1640: Dover, Hampton, Exeter, and Strawbery Banke. All the communities had something in common: long, hard workdays for everyone.

Even when the village was built, the men's work was not finished. They hunted for food, repaired the buildings and the walls of the forts, and defended the settlements from attack.

The women often worked alongside the men, helping with repairs. They also cooked the food, tended to the children, sewed and washed the clothing, made candles, and took care of the gardens.

A girl brings cows home from the pasture. From an early age, colonial children were expected to help their parents with chores.

Children took on responsibility at an early age. By the time they were school-age, settlement children were tending the gardens and working alongside their parents. Until a school and a teacher could be provided, children were taught reading and writing by their parents. At that time, it was considered more important for boys to read and write than for girls, but some families felt reading and writing was equally important for both sons and daughters.

Establishing settlements was only the beginning of the hardships for the settlers. Only after years of war did New Hampshire truly prosper and grow.

Chapter Three

Decades of Conflict

During the early years of New Hampshire's settlement, the English settlers and the Indians got along together reasonably well. They shared the land with little conflict. The settlers traded tools, iron pots, and knives for fur pelts. The Indians taught the settlers how to cultivate corn, which was an unfamiliar crop to the settlers. The Indians also taught the settlers how to build canoes.

But as more and more settlers arrived and began to displace the Indians from the land that had been their home for generations, many Indians became resentful and hostile. The first bloodshed was a conflict between a group of Indians and the English settlers. Added to this was the conflict between France and England. This conflict also affected North America, where France's goal was to establish a network of trading posts to trade for furs from the Indians. England, over time, decided it wanted settlements where colonists

The Indians offer a stag in trading with the English settlers.

could live permanently, establishing ownership of the land. Disagreements between the French and the English over who claimed ownership of this new land and all its valuable resources grew more heated. The disputes led to many years of battles and bloodshed. With battles raging throughout New England, a relatively small area of land, what affected one colony affected them all.

King Philip's War, 1675–1676

Metacom was the son of Massasoit, a Wampanoag sachem, or chief, who had helped the early English settlers. Metacom's nickname was King Philip because he behaved like a king. Metacom wanted to take back all of what he believed was his people's lands. This land included present-day southern Connecticut, New Hampshire, and western Massachusetts, which had been taken over by English settlers.

The war began when Indian warriors killed cattle owned by English settlers. The settlers responded by killing one of the Indians. Metacom declared war. Many groups of Indians banded with Metacom's forces and ambushed a group of English soldiers near Brookfield,

Indian and English soldiers meet in combat during King Philip's War.

Massachusetts, on September 3, 1675, killing eight of the soldiers. Metacom then took his war to the Connecticut River valley, attacking villages and farms and killing settlers along the river.

The colonists knew that they could not rely solely on professional soldiers to protect them. The men of one village frequently had to leave their homes and defend other settlements, both in New Hampshire and in neighboring colonies, from attacks by Metacom's warriors. New Hampshire and the other colonies required by law that all able-bodied men be trained as militiamen, so they could defend their colonies from such attacks. Their training was put to the test in many battles. King Philip's War was only one of many that claimed lives and destroyed villages in New Hampshire and the rest of New England.

Fighting would resume in 1689 and would continue for nearly a hundred years. One in ten colonists and thousands of Indians died before the war ended.

The French and Indian War

The French and Indian War, also known as the Seven Years' War, was actually a series of wars between the French and the English. The French and the English were fighting in Europe. But because both countries had interests in America, they fought in New England, as well.

Finally, in 1763, the French and Indian War came to an end in New England with the English claiming victory. Altogether, New England had seen nearly a hun-

During the French and Indian War, French soldiers cross the mountains in their fight against the English.

dred turbulent years. Thousands of colonists in New Hampshire and throughout New England had perished, but some of New Hampshire's citizens emerged as heroes.

New Hampshire's Heroes

Many New England colonists, both men and women, acted with great courage during decades of fighting. Two of the heroes of this period were Robert Rogers and John

New Hampshire hero John Stark addresses colonial troops as they prepare for battle against the French.

Stark, New Hampshire farmers who helped defeat the French invaders on New Hampshire soil and throughout New England during the final years of the French and Indian War.

Robert Rogers joined the army in 1775 and was given command of a company of rangers, mostly from New Hampshire, the following year. By 1778 Rogers was a major and in charge of nine companies. Rogers' Rangers, as they were called, quickly gained a reputation for sneak attacks on their French enemies, in New Hampshire and throughout New England. Rogers had nineteen rules he expected his rangers to follow, such as keeping their muskets clean and always having sixty rounds of ammunition, being able to march at a moment's notice, and marching with enough space between the rangers so that one shot could not pass through two men. These were important rules for soldiers who specialized in lightning-quick attacks.

Nighttime Attacks

John Stark, who later became known as New Hampshire's most famous soldier, was an important member of Rogers' Rangers. At one time, Stark was captured by Indians. During the time he was with them, Stark learned their language and customs. His knowledge made him a valuable member of the rangers.

Rogers' Rangers traveled under cover of darkness, quickly attacked soldiers and Indians guarding French forts such as Crown Point on Lake George, and slipped away before an alarm could be raised. They brought valuable information about the French forts back to the British army at Fort William Henry, and the French were never successful in attacking Fort William Henry as long as Rogers' Rangers were present. The Rangers' numerous attacks, including a raid on the Saint Francis Indians near Quebec and numerous raids in northern New Hampshire, routing the French from that area, helped bring the French and Indian War to a conclusion.

Results

The tactics of Rogers' Rangers greatly reduced French control over North America. Ultimately, the city of Quebec

British soldiers capture the French stronghold of Quebec, officially bringing an end to the French and Indian War.

*French and Indian soldiers ambush British troops.
Colonists did not fear such surprise attacks after the
Treaty of Paris was signed.*

fell to the British and in 1760 Montréal was also captured. The war was over. The Treaty of Paris in 1763 brought French control over Canada to an end. Canada, like New England, would be controlled by the British. The colonists in New Hampshire and the rest of New England no longer had to fear constant attacks from the French and their Indian allies.

But in a few years, New England's colonists went to war with the British, fighting for total freedom from England's control.

Chapter Four

From Revolution to Statehood

Although England ultimately won the French and Indian War, the many years of fighting had depleted its treasury. England was not bankrupt, but it did need money. To rebuild its wealth, England began to tax the thirteen colonies in America. Extra taxes were placed on goods such as tea and paper. Additionally, the colonists were expected to provide food, shelter, and supplies for British soldiers. The colonists of New Hampshire and the other New England colonies were outraged. They had suffered decades of war while fighting with the British against the French and the Indians. Now England was placing further burdens on them. The heavy taxes were grossly unfair, and the colonists were prepared to resist British tyranny.

As one of the original thirteen colonies, New Hampshire had an important part in America's war for independence, the Revolutionary War, from England. The people of New Hampshire played an active role in the struggle for independence. In New Castle, New Hampshire, in 1774, a small party of colonists swiftly took over the British fort called William and Mary. This was actually the first revolt against the British in the Colonies.

American colonists burn British stamps to protest the Stamp Act, a law that raised colonists' taxes.

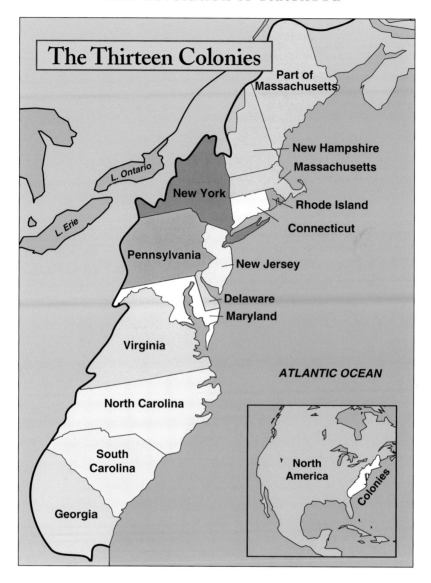

The Thirteen Colonies

Part of Massachusetts

New Hampshire

Massachusetts

L. Ontario

New York

Rhode Island

L. Erie

Connecticut

Pennsylvania

New Jersey

Delaware

Maryland

Virginia

ATLANTIC OCEAN

North Carolina

South Carolina

North America

Colonies

Georgia

Veterans Ready for Battle

The memory of the French and Indian War was still quite fresh for the New Hampshire colonists. In fact, Benning Wentworth, the last British governor of the colony, had feared future problems with the French and the Indians. As a result, he maintained a military

General George Washington commanded three New Hampshire regiments in the Revolutionary War.

unit of three militia regiments, made up of New Hampshire colonists, in case fighting broke out again. But when the colonists turned against England, Wentworth quickly left New Hampshire. The three regiments he had maintained fell under the command of General George Washington, against the British. And soldiers who had made a reputation during the French and Indian War showed their courage once again.

Among the French and Indian War veterans was New Hampshire native John Stark, who some historians say is New Hampshire's greatest war hero. Stark led troops to victory in the Battle of Bennington in present-day Vermont in 1777. This victory helped destroy England's plans to cut off the northern colonies from the southern colonies.

Minutemen

In 1775 hundreds of New Hampshire colonists rushed to Boston to join the minutemen, armed citizens who were prepared to turn out for battle at a minute's notice. Altogether, nearly twenty thousand New Hampshire colonists enlisted in the war for independence. The town of Nottingham, New Hampshire, with a population of only one thousand, contributed more officers to the war effort than any other town of its size in New England. And New Hampshire had another way to support the new country's struggle for freedom. The shipyards at Portsmouth, New Hampshire, produced three warships for America's first navy: the *Ranger,* commanded by John Paul Jones, the *America,* and the *Raleigh.*

Overall, New Hampshire's patriots did their fair share of fighting during America's war for independence from England. Finally, after seven long years of battles, the American Revolution ended with the Treaty of Paris in 1783.

New Hampshire Takes a First Step

New Hampshire took a first step that other colonies later followed. In 1776 New Hampshire was the first colony to declare itself free and independent of England. Also in 1776, New Hampshire became the first colony with a written constitution.

New Hampshire held another first in connection with the war for independence. Because New Hamp-

American and British warships battle during the Revolutionary War.

Members of the Constitutional Convention come together to discuss the future of America's constitution.

shire was the site of the first act of resistance against the British at New Castle, New Hampshire's delegates were given the honor of being the first to vote for the Declaration of Independence on July 4, 1776.

Finally, in 1788 New Hampshire became the first state to hold a Constitutional Convention and cast the deciding vote on June 21, 1788. This vote put the Constitution into effect.

A Permanent Seat of Government

New Hampshire's vote made it the ninth state in the Union. At that time, the political strength of New

Hampshire was in the southern part of the state at Portsmouth and Exeter. But farmers and pioneers in the northern part of the state, saying they were not being properly represented, soon disagreed with the government of the state. They believed that state government was putting the interests of the communities and businesses in the southern part of the state first and virtually ignoring the needs and the issues of the northern part of the state. The farmers and pioneers were so upset with the state's government in Portsmouth that they broke away from southern New Hampshire for a time. It took George Washington himself to talk the farmers and pioneers into once again becoming part of a unified state.

The problem settled itself naturally as more and more people moved into the state's interior. In New Hampshire, first as a colony and then as a state, Portsmouth was the seat of government for nearly a hundred years. But with the majority of the people moving into the western part of the state, New Hampshire needed a new capital. Concord, more centrally located on the banks of the Merrimack River, was named the new capital in 1808.

Early Days of Statehood

At the end of the 1700s, 70 percent of New Hampshire's citizens earned their living by farming, but industry experienced huge growth in the early 1800s. Over a period of ten years, the state established a dozen cotton mills. New Hampshire became an important manufacturing center, with sawmills and gristmills soon joining the state's industry. Before long New

Hampshire was a major producer of textiles, fabrics for clothing, ships' sails, draperies, and furniture upholstery. And Portsmouth remained an important navy port, hosting hundreds of clipper ships.

New Hampshire has given the United States a president, Franklin Pierce, a vice president, Henry Wilson, and a famous attorney and public speaker, Daniel Webster.

Textile mills like this one helped to make New Hampshire an important center of industry.

Modern-day New Hampshire is a picturesque state with both industry and tourism.

New Hampshire Today

Today, New Hampshire continues to thrive as a manufacturing center. Tourism is also a big industry because of the White Mountains, an area known for hiking, backpacking, skiing, snowshoeing, and a cog railway, which carries visitors to the summit of Mount Washington. New Hampshire's small but picturesque shoreline, about eighteen miles long, is also a popular tourist attraction. And the port city of Portsmouth is still a prosperous city with a large navy yard. The state also attracts tourists with its forty thousand miles of rivers and streams.

The state fish and game commission plays a major role in maintaining and increasing fish and wildlife that have lived in this area for hundreds of years. Fish and game are a major factor in the recreation business, which also attracts many visitors to New Hampshire every year. The state is also famous for its apples and for products made from the sap of maple trees, such as syrup and candy.

In recent years, New Hampshire has become involved in high-tech industries such as manufacturing computers and computer parts. The Merrimack River valley has become a center for high-tech and electrical industries.

New Hampshire has provided a sound economy for its citizens and, with a low crime rate and a low poverty level, is considered one of the safest states in which to live.

Facts About New Hampshire

State motto: Live Free or Die

State nicknames: Granite State, White Mountain State

State capital: Concord

State bird: purple finch

State tree: white birch

State flower: purple lilac

State animal: white-tailed deer

State mineral: beryl

State freshwater game fish: brook trout

State saltwater game fish: striped bass

Plant life: New Hampshire is heavily forested with elm, maple, beech, oak, pine, hemlock, and fir trees. Because of its altitude, Mount Washington has alpine plants such as alpine bearberry, dwarf cinqefoil, dwarf birch, willow, and balsam fir.

Animals: Native New Hampshire animals include porcupine, beaver, muskrat, and snowshoe hare.

Birds: Several bird species inhabiting New Hampshire are endangered. These include the arctic tern, pine marten, purple martin, peregrine falcon, osprey, and whippoorwill.

For Further Exploration

Thomas G. Aylesworth, *Northern New England: Maine, Vermont, and New Hampshire*. New York: Chelsea House, 1988. A fact-filled, heavily illustrated middle-grade volume.

Lisa Sita, *Indians of the Northeast: Traditions, History, Legends, and Life*. Milwaukee: Gareth Stevens, 2000. A colorfully illustrated volume about the life, art, culture, and customs of the Native Americans of New England.

Carter Smith, ed. *The Explorers and Settlers: A Sourcebook on Colonial America*. Brookfield, CT: Millbrook Press, 1991. Black-and-white woodcuts illustrate this narrative of the exploration and settlement of New England from 1490 to 1775.

Kathleen Thompson, *New Hampshire*. Milwaukee: Raintree, 1987. A colorfully illustrated volume well-documented with photographs. Covers the history of New Hampshire from the 1600s to the mid 1960s.

Index

Abenaki
  food of, 6, 7, 9
  homes of, 9–10
  men, 8
  women, 7
Algonquian, 6
America (warship), 35

Bennington, Battle of, 35
borders, 4

Canada, 4, 15, 28, 30
Champlain, Samuel de,
  15–16
children, 20
coastal lowlands, 4
computers, 41
Concord, 38
Connecticut, 23
Constitutional Convention,
  37
constitution, state, 36
corn, 21
Council of New England, 13

Dauphine (ship), 13–15
Declaration of Independence,
  37
Description of New England, A
  (Smith), 12

Dover, 18
du Pont, Francois Grave, 15

England
  conflict between France and,
    21–22
  explorers from, 11–13
  settlers from, 18
  taxes and, 31
  see also French and Indian
    War; Revolutionary War
Exeter, 18
explorers
  from England, 11–13
  from France, 15–16
  from Italy, 13–15

farming, 7, 38
Field, Darby, 13
food
  of Abenaki, 6, 7, 9, 21
  of Paleo-Indians, 5–6
Fort William Henry, 28
France
  conflict between England
    and, 21–22
  explorers from, 15–16
  Indians and, 16
  see also French and Indian
    War

Picture Credits

Cover photo: © Hulton/Archive by Getty Images

© Bettmann/CORBIS, 22

© Jonathan Blair/CORBIS, 5

© CORBIS, 23

© Kevin Fleming/CORBIS, 40

© Hulton/Archive by Getty Images, 34

Chris Jouan, 12

Chris Jouan and Brandy Noon, 33

© North Wind Pictures, 8, 9, 14, 16, 19, 25, 26, 28, 29, 36, 37, 39

© Gianni Dagli Orti/CORBIS, 17

© Stock Montage, Inc., 32

About the Author

Sheila Wyborny and her husband, a broadcast engineer, live in Houston, Texas. They enjoy flying their Cessna aircraft to interesting weekend locations and adding to their small antique collection. Mrs. Wyborny enjoys hearing from students who have read her books.